Mandy
Made Me Do It

by Jan Weeks

illustrated by Janine Dawson

STANLEY
THORNES

The Characters

Mandy
My little brother
keeps getting me
into trouble

Tim
Mandy's little brother

Mum

The Setting

CONTENTS

CHAPTER 1

Tim the Trouble Maker

My brother's name is Tim.
He's four years old and gets
into trouble all the time.
When he gets into trouble
he always blames **me**.

"Mandy made me do it," Tim says, pointing at me.

So I get into trouble too.

Mum says I should have more sense,
as I am older.

I used to tell Tim to do things.
But that was when I was six.

I don't do it any more.
Tim can think of bad things to do
all by himself.

At breakfast he tipped the box
of cornflakes over his head.
The cornflakes went everywhere.

Then he pushed his head
into the box and said it was
his school hat.
He doesn't even go to school.

When Mum saw the mess,
she told Tim he was a naughty
boy.

He stuck out his bottom lip
and began to cry.

"Mandy made me do it," said Tim. "She told me the cornflakes were drops of rain and that I could make a big storm."

Mum made **me** clean up the mess. It was no use telling her I didn't do it. The only person she believes is Tim.

CHAPTER 2

Beds Are Not Trampolines

After I finished cleaning up,
I found Tim jumping up and down
on his bed. Mum had just made it.

The pillow was on the floor
and the cover was crumpled.

15

"This is my trampoline,"
Tim said.

"You'll get into trouble,"
I answered. "Mum told you not
to jump on the bed."

Tim began to jump higher.

"I bet I can touch the ceiling," he said. "Whee! This is fun!"

Tim did a star jump. Then he fell off the bed and landed on his nose. He started to cry.

He cried louder and louder.
Mum came running into the room
and picked him up.

"Now what have you done?"
she asked, looking at his red nose.

"Mandy made me do it," Tim sobbed.
"She told me I was Superman.
She told me to jump off the bed."

Mum told Tim not to listen to me. He had to think for himself.

Then she showed me her angry face.

CHAPTER  3

The Next Day

I was brushing my teeth.
Tim came into the bathroom.
He had his boat in his hand.

"What are you doing?" I asked.

"Mum said I had to clean my teeth," said Tim.

He put the plug in the sink
and turned on the tap.

Tim put his boat in the water. He started singing, "Row, row, row your boat, gently down the stream."

I went to get dressed for school.
When I came back the sink
was overflowing. Tim was standing
in a pool of water.

Mum came in.

"Just look at you, Tim," Mum said.
"You're soaking wet!"

"Mandy made me do it," Tim said. "She told me my boat was a big ship sailing on the ocean. She said to make waves in the water."

"If Mandy told you to fly to the moon, would you do that too?" Mum asked.

Tim nodded his head and said
he would. He did everything I
told him. Then he smiled at me.

I was getting really tired of Tim.

CHAPTER

Visitors

On Thursday our aunt and uncle
were coming to visit. They live
a long way away and we hadn't
seen them for a long time.

"I want you both on your best behaviour," said Mum.

Mum made a chocolate cake.

On the way home from school,
she stopped at the supermarket.

She bought some strawberries
to put on top of the cake.

"I love strawberries," Tim said.
He was sitting in the back seat
of the car with the strawberries
on his lap. "Strawberries are my
favourite food."

"Just don't squash them,"
Mum said.

Mum put the strawberries
in the fridge. When she went
to use them, they had gone.

Tim was sitting on the floor
with the empty box.
His mouth was red and he had
strawberry juice all over his face.

"Mandy made me do it," Tim said. "She told me the strawberries were magic. She said if I ate them everyone would give me presents."

I knew what I'd like to give him and it wasn't a present.

Mum sent Tim to his room.
He was to stay there until she
told him to come out.

Big Trouble

Mum was talking to our aunt and uncle. They were having a good chat.

I went out into the garden
with a packet of balloons.
I wanted to make some water bombs

I had to push the balloon over
the end of the hose, and then
tie a knot to keep the water in.
It was a bit tricky.

I could see Tim watching me. It would be great to throw one at him.

Then my friend Paul came over.
He asked me to come and look
at his Dad's new car.

When I came back, Tim was in **big** trouble. He had climbed out of his bedroom window to make a water bomb.

As he turned the water on, his balloon flew off. Water sprayed all over the garden.

Just then, Mum and Aunt Beth
stepped into the garden.
Both of them were sprayed
with water. Boy, were they angry!

My aunty's new dress was soaking wet.

Mum was wearing the angriest face I'd ever seen.

"Who are you going to blame
this time?" Mum asked Tim.
"You can't blame Mandy.
She wasn't here."

"It was Daddy," he answered.
"He made me do it."

And Dad was at work.

GLOSSARY

behaviour
the way we act

blame
to say someone did
something wrong

chat
to talk to a friend

crumpled
creased and not smooth

favourite
the one I like best

overflow
when it is so full
that it spills

soaking
very very wet

sprayed
a fine stream of water

supermarket
a big shop where
you buy food

trampoline
for jumping and
tumbling

Jan Weeks

Jan Weeks has written many poems, plays, songs and stories for children. She is an experienced teacher with a particular interest in the development of sound reading skills and the promotion of literature. Jan is married, has three sons and lives in Sydney, Australia.

Janine Dawson

Janine loves to draw. In fact she loves to draw a lot — and swim, but never at the same time. She lives in Sydney, Australia, with her daughter, two cats and a nervous goldfish.